D1283655

AMY CONEY BARRETT

AMY CONEY BARRETT

Reshaping the Supreme Court

Heather E. Schwartz

Lerner Publications ◆ Minneapolis

Lerner Publications Company
An imprint of Lerner Publishing Group, Inc.
241 First Avenue North
Minneapolis, MN 55401 USA

For reading levels and more information, look up this title at www.lernerbooks.com.

Image credits: Graeme Jennings/Pool via AP, p. 2; Ken Cedeno/Pool via AP, p. 6; Brendan Smialowsi/Pool via AP, p. 8; Steve Petteway/Supreme Court of the United States/ Wikimedia Commons, pp. 9, 16, 30; Infrogmation of New Orleans/flickr (CC BY 2.0), p. 10; N'Awlins Contrarian/Wikimedia Commons (CC BY-SA 4.0), p. 11; Ed Uthman, MD/Wikimedia Commons (CC BY-SA 3.0), p. 12; REUTERS/Karen Pulfer Focht/Alamy Stock Photo, p. 13; Michael Fernandes/Wikimedia Commons (CC BY-SA 3.0), p. 14; VWEAA/Wikimedia Commons (CC BY-SA 4.0), p. 18; Official White House Photo by Andrea Hanks/Wikimedia Commons, p. 21; AP Photo/Charles Dharapak, p. 23; Wikimedia Commons (public domain), p. 25; Rachel Malehorn/Wikimedia Commons (CC BY 3.0), p. 27; Official White House Photo by Andrea Hanks/flickr, pp. 32, 39; Official White House Photo by Shealah Craighead/flickr, p. 33; Kevin Dietsch/Pool via AP, p. 36; Senate Television via AP, p. 38; Oliver Contreras/Sipa USA via AP Images, p. 40. Cover: Caroline Brehman/Pool via Xinhua/Alamy Stock Photo.

Main body text set in Rotis Serif Std 55 Regular. Typeface provided by Adobe Systems.

Library of Congress Cataloging-in-Publication Data

Names: Schwartz, Heather E. author.
Title: Amy Coney Barrett : reshaping the Supreme Court / Heather E. Schwartz.
Description: Minneapolis, MN : Lerner Publications, 2022 | Series: Gateway biographies | Includes bibliographical references and index. | Audience: Ages 9–14 | Audience: Grades 4–6 | Summary: "Amy Coney Barrett was nominated for the Supreme Court by President Donald Trump and confirmed in October 2020. Learn about her background, her time as a law professor at Notre Dame, and how she is likely to shape the Court"– Provided by publisher.
Identifiers: LCCN 2021003082 (print) | LCCN 2021003083 (ebook) | ISBN 9781728438368 (library binding) | ISBN 9781728438375 (ebook)
Subjects: LCSH: Barrett, Amy Coney–Juvenile literature. | Judges–United States–Biography– Juvenile literature. | Women judges–United States–Biography–Juvenile literature. | United States. Supreme Court–Officials and employees–Biography–Juvenile literature.
Classification: LCC KF8745.B39 S39 2021 (print) | LCC KF8745.B39 (ebook) | DDC 347.73/2634 [B]–dc23

LC record available at https://lccn.loc.gov/2021003082
LC ebook record available at https://lccn.loc.gov/2021003083

Manufactured in the United States of America
1-49663-49583-4/26/2021

TABLE OF CONTENTS

Amy Coney Barrett met with senators at the US Capitol in Washington, DC, in October 2020.

Amy Coney Barrett had risen from law student to federal judge. In October 2020 she had a chance to be confirmed as an associate justice for the US Supreme Court. But first, she would answer questions from US senators in a series of hearings. The hearings were designed to ensure she was qualified to sit on the court.

On the first day of hearings on October 12, Barrett addressed the Senate. She thanked President Donald Trump, who had nominated her to the court, and others who supported her nomination. She spoke about her family, including her husband and seven children. All but her youngest child sat behind her, listening while she gave each family member a moment in the spotlight.

As Barrett ended her address, she explained how her family influences all of her legal decisions. "When I write an opinion resolving a case, I read every word from the perspective of the losing party," she said. "I ask myself how I would view the decision if one of my children was the party that I was ruling against. Even though I would not like the result, would I understand that the decision was fairly reasoned and grounded in law? That is the standard I set for myself in every case, and it is the standard I will follow as long as I am a judge on any court."

Barrett would become the fifth woman to serve on the US Supreme Court. She would also become the first mother of school-age children on the court. But before that, she had several more days of hearings and many tough questions to answer.

Barrett speaks at her confirmation hearing on October 13.

WOMEN ON THE COURT

Four women sat on the US Supreme Court before Trump nominated Barrett to replace Associate Justice Ruth Bader Ginsburg. Ginsburg was nominated by President Bill Clinton in 1993. She served until her death on September 18, 2020.

The first woman on the US Supreme Court was Sandra Day O'Connor. She was nominated by President Ronald Reagan in 1981. She retired in 2006 after twenty-five years on the court.

President Barack Obama nominated Sonia Sotomayor in 2009. She became the first Latina Supreme Court justice. The next year Obama nominated Elena Kagan, who was confirmed. She had worked as a lawyer and professor and helped form public policy at the White House from 1995 to 1999.

From left: Sandra Day O'Connor, Sonia Sotomayor, Ruth Bader Ginsburg, and Elena Kagan

Beginnings to Build On

Born on January 28, 1972, Amy Vivian Coney grew up in Old Metairie, a suburb of New Orleans, Louisiana. She has five younger sisters and one younger brother. Her father, Michael Coney, was an attorney for Shell Oil Company. Her mother, Linda Coney, was a high school French language teacher. She later said her parents helped shape her life. "My parents modeled for me and my six siblings a life of service, principal, faith, and love," she said.

Old Metairie is known for its beautiful houses, including some that are more than one hundred years old.

The Coney family was Catholic and belonged to People of Praise, a close-knit Christian community. Amy's large extended family was also a big part of her life. Family vacations included aunts, uncles, grandparents, and cousins who felt more like siblings to Amy.

Amy attended St. Catherine of Siena Catholic School. Her parents and teachers supported her as a student. Amy's father told her that girls could do anything boys could do. The message stuck with her.

Amy attended St. Mary's Dominican High School. Her grandmother, mother, and aunts had attended the school. She learned about social justice issues from one of her teachers there. Amy also was class vice president.

St. Mary's Dominican High School

Coney graduated in 1990 and went to Rhodes College in Memphis, Tennessee. She majored in English literature and minored in French language. She joined clubs, including a Catholic student association and a mock trial group that acted out legal proceedings. She worked as an adviser for her fellow students. And she sat on the student honor council. Student honor councils make decisions about students who may have violated the school's honor code. Coney took her role

Rhodes College started in Clarksville, Tennessee, in 1848 and moved to the Memphis campus (*pictured*) in 1925.

This portrait of Barrett hangs in the Rhodes Student Hall of Fame.

Joyce S. Shin 1994

Amy V. Coney 1994

seriously. "You have the power to affect someone's life," she said. "You want to be absolutely sure you're doing the right thing by that person."

Coney took her classwork seriously too. At Rhodes she joined Phi Beta Kappa, an academic honor society. Her professors chose her as the English department's most outstanding graduate. She graduated with high honors with a bachelor of arts degree in English literature in 1994.

After graduation, Coney considered becoming a teacher like her mother. But she was inspired by her father's law career too. She decided to study law so she could build a career shaping society. Coney chose Notre Dame Law School in Indiana. She had earned a scholarship to go there, but that wasn't her only reason for picking Notre Dame. "I really wanted to choose a place where I felt like I was not going to be just educated as a lawyer," she said. "I wanted to be in a place where I felt like I would be developed and inspired as a whole person."

During law school, Coney was executive editor of the *Notre Dame Law Review* journal and earned the Colonel

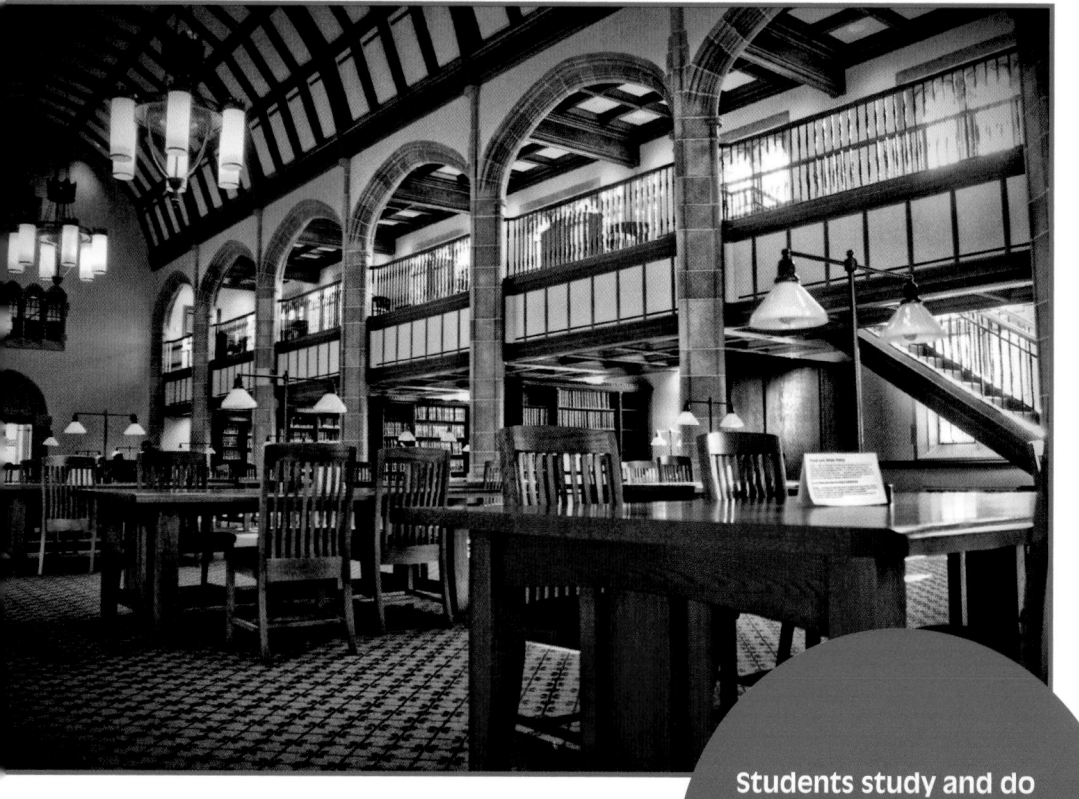

Students study and do research at the Kresge Law Library at the University of Notre Dame.

William J. Hoynes Award as the top student in her class. It was the school's highest honor. In her studies, Coney was drawn to a legal approach called originalism. It is based on interpreting the US Constitution as it would have been understood when it was originally written. She also became interested in civil rights and how the government protects them.

Coney graduated with high academic honors in 1997. Her success and achievements in school put her on a path toward a high-profile legal career.

Starting Out

After graduating from Notre Dame, Coney clerked for Judge Laurence Silberman of the United States Court of Appeals for the District of Columbia Circuit. Clerks do legal research, write opinions, and take on many other duties to help judges. Silberman recommended Coney to US Supreme Court associate justice Antonin Scalia, who was famous for his conservative legal opinions. The following year, Coney clerked for Scalia.

Like Coney, Scalia believed in originalism and in limiting the role of the federal government. Coney said she felt as if she knew Scalia before she met him because she had read and enjoyed so many of his legal opinions. "More than the style of his writing, though, it was the content of Justice Scalia's reasoning that shaped me," she said. "His judicial philosophy was straightforward.

Antonin Scalia served on the Supreme Court from 1986 until his death in 2016.

A judge must apply the law as it is written, not as the judge wishes it were."

As Scalia's clerk, Coney was responsible for helping him analyze some of the nation's most difficult cases. While Scalia made final decisions about legal rulings, Coney's position came with a lot of responsibility. She gathered additional information for Scalia to consider, debated issues with him, and offered her opinions.

Coney's talent for legal work shone as she worked with clerks of other Supreme Court justices. Traci Lovitt clerked for Associate Justice Sandra Day O'Connor, and Lovitt got to know Coney well. Lovitt admired Coney's legal curiosity and ability to make sense of complex issues. "She was one of the only, maybe the only clerk that year who had the respect of everyone, regardless of chamber, regardless of legal philosophy," Lovitt said. "She was admired by everyone."

THE SUPREME COURT

The Supreme Court is the highest court in the United States. It is made up of nine justices who serve without term limits. When a justice retires or dies, the president nominates a replacement who then must be approved by the US Senate.

Supreme Court justices decide major cases that affect the whole nation. They listen to lawyers from both sides of each case. They consider what is legal and illegal by interpreting the US Constitution. Each justice votes to determine the court's decision in a case. The majority wins.

If a vote is not unanimous, the justices have a chance to explain their different opinions. One justice writes the majority opinion, which represents those who won the vote. Another writes the dissenting opinion. This explains why one or more justices disagreed with the majority.

In 1999 Coney joined Miller, Cassidy, Larroca & Lewin, a Washington, DC, law firm. That year she married Jesse Barrett, a lawyer who attended Notre Dame Law School. The two had more than their careers in common. They both wanted a large family and were inspired by a couple they interviewed before their wedding who encouraged them to adopt.

In 2001 Miller, Cassidy, Larroca & Lewin joined Baker Botts, an international law firm. At Baker Botts, she wrote letters to judges, conducted research, and was second chair in a jury trial, helping to make the process run smoothly. In 2001 she left the firm to take her career in a new direction. She decided to merge two careers she loved—law and teaching. She became a professor at George Washington University Law School. That year she had her first child, Emma.

Amy Coney Barrett with her husband in 2018

BUSH V. GORE

Barrett was with Baker Botts during the 2000 US presidential election. It was so close that it did not have a clear winner. In the race between Republican George W. Bush and Democrat Al Gore, it all came down to Florida. The winner of the state would become president.

The vote count in Florida was extremely close and gave a slight edge to Bush. After several recounts and court cases, the dispute reached the US Supreme Court. The court ruled to end the recount, and Bush became president in January 2001.

Bush v. Gore is one of the most famous legal disputes in US history. Barrett worked on the case in Florida with Baker Botts. She did research and helped write documents for the Republican legal team.

In 2002 Barrett became an assistant professor at Notre Dame Law School. At thirty, she was close in age to her students. She wore glasses because she thought they made her look older and more imposing. More important, she took her job seriously. While leading debates, she made sure students respected one another.

She taught complicated legal ideas in simple ways to help her students better understand how the law affected real people. And she cared about her students' personal lives as well as their work in the classroom. She encouraged them to consider carefully why they wanted to be lawyers.

Family Life

Barrett's career was taking off. Meanwhile, her family was growing. Juggling a career and parenting made life more challenging, but her husband was a partner she could depend on. The couple shared chores such as cooking meals and making doctor's appointments for Emma. Barrett's workplace was accommodating to mothers. She kept a toy box in her office so Emma could entertain herself, and Barrett knew her daughter was welcome in meetings if necessary. When Emma was still small, her father's aunt began providing childcare for the couple so they could continue their careers and grow their family.

Barrett and her husband discussed having seven children, but they landed on five as the ideal number. Soon after Emma was born, they started to adopt a child from Haiti. After their second daughter, Tess, was born, Vivian came from Haiti to join the family in 2005. Vivian had been underfed and, at fourteen months, she was about the size of a newborn baby. She was weak, and doctors couldn't tell if she would ever walk or speak.

Next, a son, Liam, was born, and the couple decided to adopt again. While the adoption of their son, John Peter, was moving ahead, they learned that Barrett was pregnant again! Juliet brought the family to six children, one more than they'd planned for. "I just thought, OK, well, if life's really hard, at least it's short," Barrett joked. "But I thought, what greater thing can you do than raise children?"

The couple soon added one more child to the mix. Benjamin was born with Down syndrome. He needed special care and was in the intensive care unit of the hospital. The family was overjoyed when he was able to come home.

Amy Coney Barrett, Jesse Barrett, and six of their children meet with Donald Trump and his wife Melania Trump at the White House in September 2020.

THE BARRETT KIDS

Barrett gave an update on her children at her Supreme Court confirmation hearing in 2020. She said Emma was in college and considering a law career. Vivian was an athlete who had no trouble talking and expressing herself. Tess loved liberal arts subjects and math.

She called John Peter "happy-go-lucky," and said Liam was "smart, strong, and kind." At the age of ten, Juliet was already writing essays and short stories. Of Benjamin, Barrett said, "He is the unanimous favorite of the family."

While her family expanded, Barrett continued working hard and moving her legal career forward. She started to become known for her strong religious views. During a speech at Notre Dame Law School in 2006, she said her legal career was part of "building a kingdom of God." Critics worried that Barrett meant she would put religion first instead of following the law when making decisions. Privately, she continued her membership in People of Praise. The media reported that the organization had conservative religious values, including support for traditional gender roles and limiting marriage to unions between men and women.

Getting Noticed

As a professor at Notre Dame, Barrett made her positions on controversial issues clear. In 2012 she signed a statement criticizing President Obama's Affordable Care Act (ACA). The ACA required certain health insurance plans to cover the costs of birth control. Barrett opposed this because some religions do not support birth control, and she said the ACA could violate the religious freedoms of business owners who paid for their employees' insurance.

President Obama signs the ACA into law in March 2010.

In 2015 Barrett signed a letter to Catholic officials. It talked about human life starting at the moment a woman became pregnant, which highlighted Barrett's stance against abortion. The letter also said that a family started with a commitment between a man and a woman. Many people took this to mean she did not support same-sex marriage.

In early 2017 Barrett wrote an essay for the *Notre Dame Law Review* journal. In the essay, she criticized a 2015 US Supreme Court decision that saved the ACA from being abolished. She had especially strong criticism for Chief Justice John G. Roberts Jr., author of the court's majority opinion.

Barrett was getting national attention for her strong views. That attention went all the way to the president of the United States. Her essay about the ACA worried those who feared many Americans would lose their health insurance without the law. It appealed to Trump, however, who was committed to ending the program. In May 2017 Trump nominated Barrett for the US Court of Appeals for the Seventh Circuit.

Barrett's confirmation hearings took place in September. US senators asked questions to determine whether her strong religious views might have too much influence on her legal decisions. Some felt she wouldn't be able to separate her personal and professional beliefs. She might make decisions that would take away certain rights, such as the right for same-sex couples to marry and the right to access abortion services.

Barrett listens to a question during her confirmation hearing for the court of appeals in 2017.

Prof. Amy Coney Barrett

Senator Diane Feinstein of California said that religion and law are very different. She expressed concern about Barrett's commitment to religious dogma, or formal beliefs. "When you read your speeches, the conclusion one draws is that the dogma lives loudly within you," Feinstein said. "And that's of concern when you come to big issues that large numbers of people have fought for, for years in this country."

Barrett told senators that she would not allow personal beliefs to influence her duties as a federal judge. She said that she didn't believe it would be lawful to use her personal opinions in that way. In October, Barrett was confirmed to the court of appeals by a vote of 55–43.

THE US COURT OF APPEALS FOR THE SEVENTH CIRCUIT

The US Court of Appeals for the Seventh Circuit has fourteen judges who decide appeals, or requests to reverse decisions, from lower courts within the Seventh Circuit. The court serves Illinois, Indiana, and Wisconsin. The United States has thirteen federal courts of appeals. Decisions made by US courts of appeals can be appealed again. Those cases might go on to the US Supreme Court, the highest court in the nation.

Seventh Circuit Judge

Barrett's new position as a judge came with a lengthy trip to work. A few days a week, she traveled about 100 miles (161 km) from her home in South Bend, Indiana, to Chicago, Illinois. Her work on the Seventh Circuit bench gave her more opportunities to interpret the law on major issues facing the nation, including abortion rights, gun rights, and immigration.

In 2018 the Indiana legislature passed laws that created obstacles and extra requirements for access to abortion services. The Seventh Circuit ruled that these laws were unconstitutional. Barrett and other judges

Barrett's Seventh Circuit opinions brought increased scrutiny to her judicial philosophy.

dissented, saying the laws should have gone into effect. Throughout her legal career, Barrett's opinions and rulings have shown support for government oversight of reproductive health-care decisions that many others feel should be private.

In 2019 Barrett dissented in a gun rights case. The court's majority opinion held that people convicted of felonies did not have the right to own guns. Barrett, however, believed that the law was too broad and that judges should consider whether an individual posed a risk of violence. Her legal opinion aimed to protect and extend gun rights at a time when many people in the United States wanted to limit them.

That year the Seventh Circuit decided a college campus sexual assault case. Barrett sided with a student who was suspended from school for an alleged sexual assault and then lost career opportunities. She wrote that the school's process was not fair and discriminated against the student because he was male. The court's decision went in the male student's favor and made it easier for students accused of sexual assaults to sue their schools.

In June 2020 the Seventh Circuit stopped a new Trump administration policy that would have put legal immigrants' lives in jeopardy. According to the policy, immigrants who received food aid or other government assistance for more than a year could be barred from permanently living and working in the US. Barrett dissented. She wrote that the policy was legal. Her opinion took a hard line that many felt was unfair to immigrants in the US who might need assistance to survive.

Not all of Barrett's votes, decisions, and legal opinions were considered controversial. But her record on the Seventh Circuit showed she had conservative opinions about many issues and supported Republican Party policies. Powerful Republicans with similar views were watching, including Trump. Barrett's appointment to the US Court of Appeals for the Seventh Circuit was a lifetime position. But only three years into the job, another opportunity arose.

Supreme Court Nomination

On September 18, 2020, Ruth Bader Ginsburg died after serving on the US Supreme Court for twenty-seven years.

DOUBLE STANDARD?

In March 2016, President Obama nominated Merrick Garland to the US Supreme Court. At the time, Republicans controlled the Senate, and they blocked Garland's confirmation. They said it was too close to the upcoming presidential election, which was about eight months away.

When Trump nominated Barrett, Republicans still controlled the Senate. This time, with a Republican president in office, they took a different approach. With the presidential election less than two months away, they rushed to confirm Trump's pick.

Many Democrats saw this as a double standard. But Republicans claimed the real issue in both cases was control of the Senate. They said that in an election year, the party that controlled the Senate traditionally refused to confirm a Supreme Court justice from the other party.

Barrett was on Trump's list of potential replacements. Eight days later, he nominated her to the Supreme Court.

The nomination was controversial. The US presidential election was less than two months away. The media reported that Ginsburg's dying wish had been for a new president to fill the Supreme Court vacancy. And Barrett was known for views that directly opposed Ginsburg's.

Trump went ahead with Barrett's nomination with support from other conservative Republicans. He wanted to be sure his pick was on the court before the 2020 election. If he wasn't declared the election winner, he planned to challenge the results in court. If a case reached the US Supreme Court, Trump expected that any justice he'd chosen would decide in his favor.

Ruth Bader Ginsburg

A WORLD IN PERIL

Barrett's Supreme Court nomination and confirmation hearings occurred during one of the world's worst pandemics. In late 2019, a new coronavirus began spreading in China. By 2020 the coronavirus, which causes the disease COVID-19, had arrived in the United States.

In public, Trump took a relaxed attitude toward the threat. Critics said he didn't take the disease seriously enough. By April the death toll in the United States from COVID-19 was the highest in the world.

Health experts began advising people to wear face masks when they left home to prevent spreading the disease. Trump downplayed the importance of masks and rarely wore one publicly, and many Americans followed his example. Federal health officials urged people to stay home and to keep their distance from one another in public. But Trump felt that circumstances in each state were different and that state leaders should make their own health and safety rules.

The fight against COVID-19 turned into a political battle. Democrats claimed they were following the advice of scientists and health experts, while some Republicans said they were standing up for freedom against an overreaching government. Most Democratic leaders supported shutting down nonessential businesses and pushed for strong masking and social distancing rules. Many Republican leaders resisted shutdowns and said people should make their own decisions about their health. Meanwhile, the disease continued to devastate the country. In March 2021, the federal government announced that more than five hundred thousand people in the US had died from COVID-19.

Due to the threat of COVID-19, Washington, DC, officials had banned gatherings of more than fifty people. Despite the ban, Trump held a nomination ceremony for Barrett in the White House Rose Garden on September 26. More than two hundred people gathered to celebrate, including Justice Scalia's widow, Republican US senators, and Barrett's family. People around the country were watching and listening too.

When Barrett spoke, she stressed that if confirmed to the court, she would be unbiased in serving the American people. In her remarks, she made a direct connection to Scalia's mentorship. "His judicial philosophy is mine too: A judge must apply the law as written," she said. "If confirmed, I would not assume that role for the sake of those in my own circle, and certainly not for my own sake. I would assume this role to serve you."

The crowd sat closely packed together as they listened to Barrett speak. They mingled in the Rose Garden and inside the White House. Many people did not wear face masks or practice social distancing.

With Trump looking on, Barrett addresses her supporters at the Rose Garden.

In early October, COVID-19 began spreading at the highest levels of the US government. First, a top adviser to the president tested positive for the virus. A few hours later, the media reported that Trump and his wife had it too. Within the week, many more people who had attended the Rose Garden ceremony had COVID-19. They included two Republican senators and the president of the University of Notre Dame. Barrett's nomination ceremony became known as a super-spreader event where COVID-19 spread rapidly. The media reported that Barrett had contracted and recovered from the disease earlier that year. She most likely gained a strong resistance to COVID-19 and avoided catching it again in September and October.

With the virus spreading among top US leaders, some questioned whether it was safe for the Senate to hold

Barrett's confirmation hearings. The two sick senators might be too ill to vote. It looked as if the Rose Garden ceremony could derail Barrett's confirmation to the Supreme Court.

Supreme Court Justice

On October 12, 2020, the US Senate began Barrett's Supreme Court confirmation hearings. Many senators wanted to hear about her views on the ACA and abortion. Senators asked if Barrett would remove herself from the case if a presidential election challenge reached the Supreme Court. By removing herself, she would not be forced to choose between loyalty to the law and loyalty to Trump. Barrett said that she couldn't make a decision about removing herself from a case that didn't yet exist.

The hearings went on for four days, and Barrett answered questions for hours. No matter what senators thought of her answers, many observers expected that Republicans would vote to confirm Barrett and that Democrats would vote against her. Feelings ran high on both sides.

During the hearings, Barrett talked about her family. She recalled how inspired she was by the women who'd served on the Supreme Court before her. She called Sandra Day O'Connor "a model of grace and dignity throughout her distinguished tenure on the court," and noted that no one could ever replace Ginsburg.

REPLACING GINSBURG

Some people applauded Trump for choosing another woman to serve on the Supreme Court after Ruth Bader Ginsburg's death. Barrett and Ginsburg have a few similarities and many opposing views. Both women built their lives on religious foundations. Barrett comes from a Catholic background, while Ginsburg was Jewish. However, Ginsburg spoke in favor of pro-choice rulings, whereas some think Barrett's antiabortion views could lead to decisions that would reverse those rulings.

Barrett made it clear that she respected Ginsburg's legacy, even though Ginsburg's views differed from her own. "I have been nominated to fill Justice Ginsburg's seat, but no one will ever take her place," Barrett said. "I will be forever grateful for the path she marked and the life she led."

Most important, she stressed her commitment to the law over personal feelings. "I chose to accept the nomination because I believe deeply in the rule of law and the place of the Supreme Court in our nation," she said. "I believe Americans of all backgrounds deserve an independent Supreme Court that interprets our Constitution and laws as they are written."

The two senators who had contracted COVID-19 at the Rose Garden event were well enough to attend the hearings and vote in favor of Barrett. On October 26, she was confirmed 52–48. At forty-eight, Barrett was the youngest woman ever seated on the Supreme Court. She is expected to serve for decades in the lifelong position.

TRANSFORMING THE COURT

American voters often divide themselves into two groups: conservative and liberal. Conservatives believe government should play a smaller role so people have more freedom to make their own choices. Conservatives are generally Republicans.

Liberals tend to believe government should be more active in enforcing equality among different groups. Liberals are usually Democrats.

Barrett was the third Trump nominee to sit on the US Supreme Court. Neil Gorsuch took his seat on April 10, 2017, and Brett Kavanaugh was seated on October 6, 2018. With three conservative justices added to the court during Trump's term, many observers expect future court decisions to favor conservative ideas and causes.

YEA 52   NAY 48

Nomination of Amy Coney Barrett,
of Indiana, to be an Associate Justice
of the United States Supreme Court

After the vote, Barrett spoke at her swearing-in ceremony at the White House. "My fellow Americans, even though we judges don't face elections, we still work for you," she said. "It is your Constitution that establishes the rule of law and the judicial independence that is so central to it."

Senators vote Amy Coney Barrett to be an associate justice of the United States Supreme Court.

Barrett became the 115th US Supreme Court justice on October 27, 2020.

Trump's challenger in the election on November 3 was former vice president Joe Biden. Counting the votes was expected to take days. Many states had passed new rules to allow more mail-in ballots so people could vote safely without exposing themselves to COVID-19. Trump said mail-in voting made it easier to cheat and encouraged his supporters to vote in person.

In many states, ballots cast in person on election day were counted first. They showed Trump leading. But as election officials counted mail-in ballots, Biden took the lead in several states where he had been behind. Trump denounced the election, claiming without evidence that the vote counting in some states he had lost was fraudulent. As Biden secured enough electoral college votes to become the next president, Trump began to file lawsuits challenging the election.

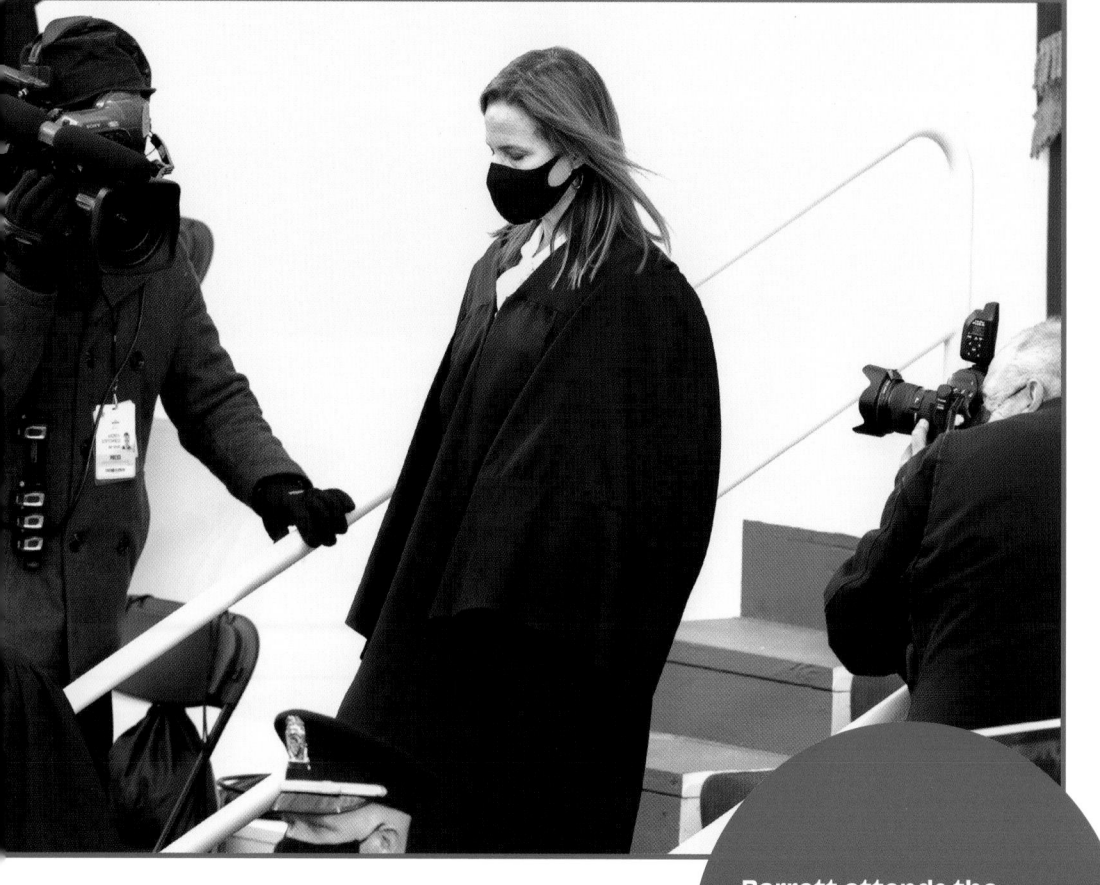

Barrett attends the inauguration of President Joe Biden in January 2021.

In December a lawsuit supporting Trump's election challenges went to the Supreme Court. It asked judges to block the certification of Pennsylvania's votes, preventing Biden from winning the state. Trump hoped the justices he'd nominated would help him overturn the election.

The court denied the request. No judge dissented, and the judges offered no further comments. Barrett proved her loyalty was to the law, not to the person who'd nominated her to the court.

Some Americans who don't agree with Barrett's views are worried about decisions she could make on important cases that may reach the Supreme Court. Her opinions will affect the country for decades. But at her swearing-in ceremony, she promised to stand for all Americans. "The oath that I have solemnly taken tonight means at its core that I will do my job without any fear or favor, and that I will do so independently of both the political branches and of my own preferences," she said.

Barrett has expressed commitment to her duty to make fair and impartial decisions. She brings a strong work ethic to her role on the Supreme Court. With many years as a Supreme Court justice ahead of her, she is poised to have a lasting and influential role.

IMPORTANT DATES

1972	Amy Vivian Coney is born.
1997	She graduates from Notre Dame Law School.
1998	She clerks for Supreme Court associate justice Antonin Scalia.
1999	She joins a Washington, DC, law firm.
	She marries Jesse Barrett.
2000	Barrett works on *Bush v. Gore*.
2002	She becomes an assistant professor at Notre Dame Law School.
2016	Donald Trump is elected president of the United States.
2017	Trump nominates Barrett to the US Court of Appeals for the Seventh Circuit, and she joins the court in October.

2020	The disease COVID-19 spreads around the world.
	Supreme Court justice Ruth Bader Ginsburg dies on September 18.
	Trump nominates Barrett to the US Supreme Court on September 26.
	She is confirmed to the US Supreme Court on October 26.
	Joe Biden wins the US presidential election.
	On December 8, the US Supreme Court turns away a Republican attempt to overturn the election results in Pennsylvania.
2021	Barrett delivers her first Supreme Court majority opinion on March 4.

SOURCE NOTES

8   Allan Smith, "Barrett Explains How Her Children Factor into Her Judicial Philosophy," NBC News, updated October 13, 2020, https://www.nbcnews.com/politics/supreme-court/live-blog/live-updates-amy-coney-barrett-confirmation-hearings-kick-n1242845/ncrd1243004#blogHeader.

10 Debbie Lord, "Read Amy Coney Barrett's Opening Statement from Monday's Supreme Court Nomination Hearing," WPXI.com, updated October 12, 2020, https://www.wpxi.com/news/trending/read-amy-coney-barretts-opening-statement-ahead-mondays-supreme-court-nomination-hearing/SYVKWELIVJEQHH2X5DCBSSZYLU/.

13 Elizabeth Dias, Rebecca R. Ruiz, and Sharon LaFraniere, "Rooted in Faith, Amy Coney Barrett Represents a New Conservatism," *New York Times*, updated March 4, 2021, https://www.nytimes.com/2020/10/11/us/politics/amy-coney-barrett-life-career-family.html.

14 Dias, Ruiz, and LaFraniere.

15–16 Susan Ferrechio, "Amy Coney Barrett Strikes Defiant Tone, Says like Scalia, She Will Be 'Fearless of Criticisms,'" *Washington Examiner*, October 12, 2020, https://www.washingtonexaminer.com/news/congress/amy-coney-barrett-strikes-defiant-tone-says-like-scalia-she-will-be-fearless-of-criticisms.

16 Salena Zito, "What Amy Coney Barrett Is like as a Sister and Fellow Supreme Court Clerk," *Washington Examiner*, October 12, 2020, https://www.washingtonexaminer.com/opinion/what-amy-coney-barrett-is-like-as-a-sister-and-fellow-supreme-court-clerk.

21 Dias, Ruiz, and LaFraniere, "Rooted in Faith."

22 Matt Hadro, "Amy Coney Barrett and 'Building the Kingdom of God,'" Catholic News Agency, September 23, 2020, https://www.catholicnewsagency.com/news/amy-coney-barrett-and-building-the-kingdom-of-god-64758.

22 Scott Stump, "Amy Coney Barrett Opens Up about Her 7 Children at Supreme Court Confirmation Hearing," *Today*, updated October 12, 2020, https://www.today.com/parents/amy-coney-barrett-talks-about-her-kids-confirmation-hearing-t194002.

25 James Crump, "'The Dogma Lives Loudly in You': Dianne Feinstein's Grilling of Trump SCOTUS Frontrunner for Her Devout Catholicism Goes Viral," *Independent* (London), September 22, 2020, https://www.independent.co.uk /news/world/americas/us-politics/amy-coney-barrett-supreme-court-diana -feinstein-ruth-bader-ginsburg-b512741.html.

32 Peter Baker and Nicholas Fandos, "Trump Announces Barrett as Supreme Court Nominee, Describing Her as Heir to Scalia," *New York Times*, updated September 28, 2020, https://www.nytimes.com/2020/09/26/us/politics/amy -coney-barrett-supreme-court.html.

34 Adam Liptak, "Justice Barrett Stressed Her Biography and the Influence Justice Antonin Scalia Had on Her," *New York Times*, updated October 12, 2020, https://www.nytimes.com/live/2020/10/12/us/amy-coney-barrett-live /judge-barrett-stressed-her-biography-and-the-influence-justice-antonin -scalia-had-on-her.

35 Tucker Higgins, "Here's What You Need to Know about Amy Coney Barrett's Supreme Court Confirmation Hearings," CNBC, updated October 12, 2020, https://www.cnbc.com/2020/10/11/amy-coney-barrett-supreme-court -confirmation-hearings-what-you-need-to-know.html.

36 Tucker Higgins, "Amy Coney Barrett Emphasizes Her Family in Confirmation Hearing Opening Statement," CNBC, October 11, 2020, https://www.cnbc .com/2020/10/11/amy-coney-barrett-emphasizes-her-family-in-opening -statement.html.

38 Maegan Vazquez, "White House Holds Swearing-In Ceremony for Amy Coney Barrett," CNN, updated October 26, 2020, https://www.cnn.com/2020 /10/26/politics/white-house-amy-coney-barrett-swearing-in/index.html.

41 Vazquez.

SELECTED BIBLIOGRAPHY

"Meet the Four Women Who Preceded Amy Coney Barrett on the Supreme Court." *USA Today*. Updated October 27, 2020. https://www.usatoday.com/in-depth/life/women-of-the-century/2020/10/26/four-women-preceded-amy-coney-barrett-us-supreme-court-sonia-sotomayor-ruth-bader-ginsburg/3710518001/.

Nuss-Warren, Dora. "Who Are Amy Coney Barrett's Children?" Moms.com. September 26, 2020. https://www.moms.com/amy-coney-barretts-children/.

"Read: Amy Coney Barrett's Opening Statement to Senate Judiciary Committee." CNN. Updated October 11, 2020. https://www.cnn.com/2020/10/11/politics/read-amy-coney-barrett-opening-statement/index.html.

Stump, Scott. "Amy Coney Barrett Opens Up about Her 7 Children at Supreme Court Confirmation Hearing." *Today*. Updated October 12, 2020. https://www.today.com/parents/amy-coney-barrett-talks-about-her-kids-confirmation-hearing-t194002.

"Supreme Court of the United States—History and Traditions." Supremecourt.gov. Accessed March 10, 2021. https://www.supremecourt.gov/about/historyandtraditions.aspx.

LEARN MORE

The Law School–University of Notre Dame
https://law.nd.edu

Levy, Debbie. *Becoming RBG: Ruth Bader Ginsburg's Journey to Justice.*
New York: Simon & Schuster, 2019.

Roland, James. *Ruth Bader Ginsburg, 2nd Edition: Iconic Supreme Court
Justice.* Minneapolis: Lerner Publications, 2021.

Sonnenborn, Liz. *The Supreme Court: Why It Matters to You.* New York:
Children's Press, 2020.

Supreme Court of the United States: Current Members
https://www.supremecourt.gov/about/biographies.aspx

The Supreme Court of the United States and the Federal Judiciary
https://www.fjc.gov/history/courts/supreme-court-united-states-and
-federal-judiciary

INDEX